Dedication

This book is dedicated to my son, **Conner Crawford**, and my daughter, **Kelsey Crawford**. You bring me more joy than I deserve. You are good and perfect gifts from our Heavenly Father. Being your dad makes me proud. I love you with an everlasting love. Thank you for being so awesome.

This book is also dedicated to my mother, **Bobbie Crawford**, who has taught me what love is all about. I hope one day I can exhibit the gift of giving the way you have expressed it throughout my life. Mom, thank you for being longsuffering. I have put you through so much, but you continued to pray more fervently and love more sacrificially. You are the best!

To my brothers, **Alan**, **Guy** and **Rich**, and my immediate family, thank you. You never gave up on me when others did. I will be forever grateful for your love and support. You're a big part of my dreams being fulfilled. Thank you for not just being my family, but also my friends when I needed them most. I love you so much.

To the people of **First Family Church**, I say thank you for your love, support and encouragement, which are second to none. I am committed to serving you, Pastor Jon, and your congregation. Our greatest days are ahead.

Acknowledgments

As with any book, it takes a great team to make all the elements come together. I want to extend my personal and sincere thanks to a number of people.

Pastor Dr. Jon Ogle—First Family Church. Thank you for being my pastor. Your leadership and guidance have impacted my life and ministry forever.

Pastor Jimmy Clark—All in The Word Ministries. Thank you for always being there for my family and me. You are not just a pastor; you are my friend. You have always encouraged me to follow my dreams. You have always spoken truth, and I thank you for that.

Pastor Jerry Howell—Destiny Christian Center. Your prophetic voice is like no other. Thank you for being my pastor and my friend when I got out of prison. Every prophetic word spoken over me is coming to pass. Thank you for your faithfulness.

Pastor Tommy Morgan—Potter's Wheel Ministries. You gave me my first opportunity as a youth pastor. Thank you for loving me and trusting in my abilities. You stood up to me when others would not. Thank you for your correction. It changed me.

Don and Janice Buttrey—You were there at the most pivotal time of my life. Your direction and unconditional love changed my course of life forever. Thank you.

Randy Richter—Law of Liberty Prison Ministry. You discipled me and taught me shortly after I came out of prison. You took a chance on me, and I will be forever grateful. Thank you for all your support and for helping me with my new start.

Tracy Allen—Thank you for your unwavering enthusiasm, your constant encouragement, and for being my best friend. You have been faithful to me for many years. I am eternally grateful.

Gina Fraga—Your gifts and talents are second to none. Thank you for finalizing the manuscript, as well as, marketing, promotion, art work and support. You're a gift to Clark Crawford Ministries.

Terri Crawford—Thank you for all the work you did on the manuscript. You never once complained about the many changes. You poured your life into making this dream of mine come true. I am forever grateful.

Sue Coffman—Without your editing abilities, this would have been a mess. Thank you for caring and your professionalism. I am very thankful to have you in my life.

Derek Nelson—Your significant financial seed made this book, as well as other ministries, a reality in my life. I will be forever grateful. Thank you!

Table of Contents

Introduction   9

Clark's Salvation   13

Clark's Journal: Angel Visitation   17

Chapter 1: From Nothing to Something   23

Chapter 2: The Glass House   27

Chapter 3: Favor in Venus   31

Chapter 4: New Life (I Thought)   35

Chapter 5: Lukewarm Brings Bondage   39

Chapter 6: Addicted to Jesus   45

Chapter 7: Love Eternal   49

Chapter 8: Fear of Failure   53

Chapter 9: Renewing Your Mind   57

Chapter 10: From Prisoner to Worshiper   61

Chapter 11: Clark Crawford Ministries   65

Introduction

Thank God I got caught with 10,000 hits of ecstasy and $40,000 in cash on September 23, 1988. This was the start of the greatest encounter I would ever experience outside of where I am today.

On January 12, 1990, I was convicted of "conspiracy to possess a controlled substance." I was given a 20-year sentence in the Texas Department of Corrections. Since I believed I had been promised 10 years of "deferred adjudicated probation" by the judge a month before, needless to say I was devastated.

When the judge read the sentence, all I could remember was my mother screaming in the courtroom. I was immediately handcuffed and taken to a holding cell outside the courtroom.

While in the holding cell, I remembered that I had always said, "I'll kill myself before I ever will go to prison." Well, God's ways are not our ways. Sometimes God will allow you to go through things that you said you never could, just to show you that with Him you can do all things. Romans 8:28 says *All things work together for good to those who love God.*

As I write this book 20 years later, I realize that my pain and suffering—caused by sin over the years—were for all the people that will be reading this book. I would not change one thing I have been through. The compassion and love I have for hurting people today are the result of the Lord Jesus Christ coming into my heart as a result of going to prison. Thank God for His healing power. He is so awesome. He has a plan for you, too. Who would ever have thought that God could use someone like me? By the grace of God I am alive today to tell my story.

He will move heaven and earth to chase you down and make His love known to you. Maybe you will not find Him in a physical prison like I did. Many are in prisons of their own making. Maybe it is abuse, anger, hate, bitterness, drugs, alcohol, pornography, gambling, divorce, a lost son or daughter, unforgiveness or just loneliness.

God is not willing that any should perish, but that all should come to repentance (2 Peter 3:9).

My prayer for you is that you will open your heart and allow God to go where no man has ever gone before. God is able to do exceedingly abundantly above all that you ask or think (Ephesians 3:20). Jesus said, *"With men this is impossible, but with God all things are possible"* (Matthew 19:26).

Nobody can ever tell me there is not a God. This is why I am so radical and on fire for my Lord and Savior. My calling is to stir the hearts of people everywhere I go. I am determined that God is going to take thousands of people with me to heaven.

I know what it is to have a heart attack and a stroke, to be totally blind from a drug overdose and to be given up for dead numerous times—yet God showed up miraculously to spare my life and heal me. I was abused by my father. My wife left me and took my children. I have been stripped of everything that I loved. Yet I love and trust God with all my heart. I know and am experiencing His grace and mercy.

You do not know what you have until it is gone. Husbands love your wives, as Christ loved the church. Spend time with your children and love people, because it can all be gone in the blink of an eye.

Now let us take the journey together so that your life may be changed forever. Who knows, you just might be saying "thank God I got caught" too!

Clark's Salvation

As a little boy I was always made to go to church. I was reared in a Methodist Church in Dallas, Texas. My brothers and I would go with our mother. I would always ask my dad why he was not going with us. This was especially puzzling since he would make us go even if we didn't feel like going on Sunday morning. He would always reply, "I know the Lord, so I don't have to go." That was the only explanation I would ever get from him.

So I was reared, "Do as I say, not as I do." No wonder I was reared with a religious spirit—always judging and being legalistic. To be honest, other than going to church to get the donuts, I hated church. It was so dead and dry. I found church very boring!

Many years went by as I became more and more hardened toward the church. No power, just religion. I had to dress a certain way, say the right things, and God forbid if I let people know how I really felt—hurt, abused, fearful, insecure, tormented and controlled (just to name a few).

On January 12, 1990, I ended up in prison. I began to get desperate. Amazing how you begin to search your heart when you are put in a situation of despair, and nobody is available to help you. It's just you and God. I stayed in the Dallas jail for a couple of months. The jail was overcrowded, and I had to wait for a bed. Therefore, I ended up having to sleep on the floor in puddles of water. Eventually I became sick from it. I was so miserable and scared. I became more desperate day by day.

Within a week or so, another inmate asked me to go with him to a church service. Well, I thought to myself, *it can't hurt anything*, so I went. Wow! The service was nothing like that religious church in which I was reared. This guy was serious about God. He was born again"while in jail and had a story to tell—and without a care of what anyone thought about him or his story. All he cared about was getting his point across and lifting the name of Jesus. He seemed to genuinely care about all of us inmates. This was a far cry from what I had seen and experienced over the years in our church. The next thing I knew, I was given a Bible, so I started reading it. Slowly but surely I began to feel different. Out of nowhere hurt, bitterness and unforgiveness were not consuming my every thought.

Over the next two months I would pray, read, and workout almost everyday. The day eventually arrived when they called my name, and I was on my way to prison. We spent a couple of hours in different holding cells. Then they brought all of us prisoners outside and chained us together by our hands, waist, and feet. They put us on the prison bus and took us to Texas' Goree Unit for classification. This was where we found out the exact prison where we were going. This is also where I would be born again—and my life would never be the same again. *Thank you Jesus!*

On March 19, 1990, in a single cell at the Goree Unit in Huntsville, Texas, I would say the "sinners prayer." No man influenced me, only the love of Jesus Christ.

Here is how it happened:

I had not received any mail in a couple of weeks. Since this day was also my birthday, I was really lonely. I wondered why everyone had abandoned me. Up until the previous couple of weeks I had been receiving mail every few days. Amazing how a piece of mail can keep you going while incarcerated! If you have a loved one, or just a friend who is locked up, let me tell you first hand, nothing is more important to an inmate than a piece of mail. You may want to consider writing a letter to that person today.

On this particular morning, I was in my cell. I began to cry uncontrollably. During that time my whole life flashed before my eyes. The brokenness became much more intense. All of a sudden I said, *"Dear Jesus, I ask you to come into my heart and save me. I repent of all my sins. I ask you to take control of my life."* My conversion was that simple. The next thing I knew, the peace of God as I know it today filled my heart. I knew beyond a shadow of a doubt that God had saved my soul. Guess what happened that afternoon? When the mail arrived, I had so much mail that it took me an hour or so to read it all. *Hallelujah to the Lamb of God.* God had held up that mail, because He knew that would be the very thing that would cause my name to be written in the Lamb's Book of Life. *Glory to God in the highest.*

As you read *Thank God I Got Caught*, my prayer is that you will have an encounter with Jesus Christ just as I did. No greater thing exists than to surrender your life to the One Who died for you. He awaits your surrender.

Clark's Journal: Angel Visitation

Thursday, February 5, 2009 (3:05pm)
I was on my way to a nursing home to minister to a man who a few days earlier had given his life to Jesus. On the way there, my brand-new ministry phone rang and a woman's voice asked me if I can return home. I started wondering how this person knew that I wasn't at home, so I asked, "Who are you?" She said, "I can't tell you that. I just want to bless you." Then I asked again, "Who are you?" She said, "If I told you, it would ruin it." So I said, "Okay" and I turned around and headed back home.

Thursday, February 5, 2009 (3:30 p.m.)
After I returned home, I sat on the front porch reading the Bible; shortly and an old blue truck pulled into the cul-de-sac and parked. As I approached the truck, I saw two women. An older lady said her name was Carolyn. She was in the driver's seat. She had bandages covering her nose and one eye. Her nose and eye were swollen, black and blue. She then introduced the second lady and said, "This is my daughter, Amie." I then asked them again, "Who are you?" She said, "We are angels from God." Then she handed me five $20 bills and said, "There is more coming." Tears began to pour down my

face. I said, "Can I give ya'll a hug?" They said, "Yes." I hugged Amie through the passenger seat window. Carolyn then got out of the truck and walked around it. She took my hand. I then prayed for them. I asked that the Lord give back good measure, pressed down and shaken together, and to bless them. Carolyn got back in the truck and drove away. Needless to say, I was awestruck.

I went into the house. I went to my room and fell on my face before God. My mind began to try and figure this out, because nothing like this had ever happened to me before. To be honest I thought people who told these kinds of stories about things like this happening were nuts. Then I realized that I had just gotten my new phone and phone number and only two people had that number. Neither of these two women was on that very short list.

Other things that puzzled me were that Carolyn
- knew I was not at home
- knew where I lived
- knew my name
- knew my brand new phone number.

More and more started entering my mind. Earlier that morning I had received an e-mail from someone who was praying that an angel would visit me and bless me that day. Also, before I got out of my bed that morning I was thinking about angels. I almost asked the Lord to let me see one, but I thought that was nonsense. Who am I kidding? God knows our thoughts. Amazing!! I had been praying that the Lord would bring finances out of hidden places—from the north, south, east, and west. I had been looking for a job, but every door had been closed. Pastors and other leaders had been praying for me. I had been absolutely broke, living off family and friends, and desperate to pay my tithe, make offerings, buy groceries, and pay for utilities. I had been working full-time in ministry—but no income had been forthcoming.

Others have said, "Clark, you are working. Behind the scenes God sees what you are doing ." In the last two weeks over 20 people have been saved. Signs and wonders have followed me everywhere I have gone. I just received three letters from people in prison. People in my church are asking me continually to pray for them. They said they want the "fire" that I have. *Glory to God in the highest; to God be the glory.* I can truly say that *I have been crucified with Christ, nevertheless I live, yet not I, but Christ in me* (Galatians 2:20). *For in Him I live and move and have my being* (Acts 17:28).

Something else that is amazing is when I told my mother what happened, she said, "Clark, I am getting chill bumps all over." If you new my mom, for her to say this, you would know this was a miracle. It gets even better!!

Friday, February 6, 2009 (6:40 a.m.)

My mother awakened me and asked if I knew about groceries on our front porch. I said, "What?" I threw on my clothes and went downstairs. To my amazement, bags and a huge basket of groceries and necessities were sitting on our front porch. I would estimate the cost of those items at $300.00. Among the things were some of my favorite foods. Unbelievable! You have to understand that I have been burdened recently because I have not been able to give my mother money nor buy groceries. I have been crying out to God to make a way where there seems to be no way. *WOW!! What an awesome God we serve.* So I went upstairs to my room and fell on my knees worshipping and praising God for what He has done. Tears flowed like rivers as I told Him how thankful I am. I told Him how much I love Him. As I sat up on my bed a bright light from the sky hit me in the eyes like you wouldn't believe. I felt the Lord saying, "My eyes are upon you." Then I turned my new phone on. I have a voice message from Carolyn, the angel, saying, "Clark, Amie & I wanted to let you know that we are shutting down our phone." Glory to God!! God Almighty had sent two angels to my home to bless me with finances and food. I will never limit God again.

Saturday, February 7, 2009 (8:05 a.m.)

This morning I woke up praying and seeking God's face for His goodness and mercy. I began to pray Philippians 4:6-7. When I finished I turned on my phone. I had a message from Amie (the angel) saying, "Clark, we have left something for you in your mailbox." I went downstairs. My mother had already brought in the groceries off the front porch. I then looked in the mailbox and found a card. This card had the scripture (Philippians 4:7), which is what I was praying this morning. On the front of the card it said, "For those HARD-TO-UNDERSTAND times." Wow, what an awesome God we serve. The card had $200.00 in 20-dollar bills in it. My mother once again confessed with her mouth, "This has to be a miracle." The Lord has showed me that He has given me proof with the card signed by Amie & Carolyn—the angels—as well as three voice messages from them. He wants people to KNOW what He is doing in the earth today. This is just the beginning. WITH GOD ALL THINGS ARE POSSIBLE AND NOTHING SHALL BE IMPOSSIBLE!!

Monday, February 9, 2009 (5:25 a.m.)

Once again, I awoke to $300.00 worth of groceries on the front porch as well as another envelope with a card and $100.00 in $20's in the mailbox. The card was signed, "God's Angels". Here was more proof!! I turned my phone on and had three more voice messages from Carolyn & Amie, the angels.

The last voice message said, "Hi Clark, I just called to tell you not to worry now. Jesus has you in His hands. He is going to take care of you. You are going to be richly blessed. If you need anything you can call me and Amie."

Chapter 1
From Nothing to Something

After 20 years of knowing the Lord, I am now instructed to write *Thank God I Got Caught*. My intention is twofold. First and foremost I want to bring honor and glory to my personal Lord and Savior Jesus Christ. Second, I hope that others will realize that if they will learn from my many mistakes, they will save themselves much pain and suffering. This is not to say that we will not have hardships, because Hebrews 5:8 says that though Jesus was the Son of God, He learned obedience through the things which He suffered. We will go through suffering as Christians, but we must realize that it will make us stronger and show us what is in our own hearts. We do not know who we truly are until the pressure is on.

I could have saved myself much heartache and turmoil in my own life if I had understood this one truth. If you will work with God and not against Him, you will get your victories in each lesson much more quickly. You will not have to go around the same old mountain time and time again. Until you pass each test, God will bring you back again and again to the same place. The good news is that once you pass each test, you get promoted to the next one. *Hallelujah to the Lamb of God.*

My life changed when I realized that the devil could not do anything without God's permission. God is sovereign. He rules the universe and the world. He will not allow any more suffering than you are able to bear (1 Corinthians 10:13)! Everything in your life is working for good (Romans 8:28). He is preparing you for something great and awesome—as Ephesians 3:20 says, *now unto Him who is able to do exceedingly abundantly above all that you ask or think, according to the power that works in you.*

The chief sin of the Israelites was that they limited the Holy One of Israel (Psalm 78:41). Do not limit God. The Bible says that with God all things are possible. He has been so good to me. As I look back over my life, He has never left me nor forsaken me. It is only because of Him that I am alive today to tell my story. I have never been as happy as I am today. When you totally surrender your life to Jesus Christ, you can rest assured that your life will turn out better than you ever expected.

The Lord has made me what I always wanted to be. I am patient, kind, loving, giving and faithful. Until I allowed the Spirit of God to work in my heart, I was the most selfish person you could know. I had hate, anger, resentment, bitterness, wanted revenge and had every evil work in my heart. I tried everything in my own strength to change, but I now know the only One who can heal— and His name is Jesus Christ. We all must make a decision to surrender our lives totally to the Lordship of Jesus Christ. Then and only then was I delivered from drug addiction, alcoholism, sex addiction, gambling addiction, abuse and other works of darkness.

Now I love myself in a healthy way. God said that He created me in His image. Scripture says that I am fearfully and wonderfully made; marvelous are His works (Psalm 139:14). You are awesome, and God has a great plan for your life, too. He desires for you to be happy and whole. Give God a chance and watch what He does in you and through you. You can love God with all your heart, mind, soul and strength. You can love yourself in a healthy way. Then you can love your neighbor as yourself. You can love your enemies and even pray for them. It is amazing how God will give you these abilities and gifts. You will begin to see that God has used the enemy to make you into His image.

God brings hateful people into your life to teach you how to love and forgive. You prayed for patience, so understand why God brings those impatient people into your life. You prayed to God to use you, so don't question Him anymore about why you are the only Christian at your job. See through God's eyes. He is working all the time on your behalf. He is working behind the scenes, putting all the pieces together. Have faith in God because without faith it is impossible to please Him (Hebrews 11:6). Faith without works is dead (James 2:26). God is stretching you, refining you, pruning you so you can produce more fruit (John 15:2). God knows exactly what He is doing. Thank God He has not answered your prayers in your time. I look back over the years and realize that many times if my prayers would have been answered when I wanted them answered, it would have been a disaster. Thank God He is in control and I am not.

There is an appointed time for everything; though it tarries, wait for it, for it shall surely come (Habakkuk

2:3). Let God put all the pieces together and bring it to pass, or it will not be His divine destiny and plan for your life. Do not stop short of your miracle. It is right around the corner. You are one day closer. *Hallelujah!* In the wilderness you are conformed into the image of Christ. Shadrach, Meshach and Abednego experienced God in the fiery furnace (Daniel 3:6). God was there with them; they were not touched by the fire and came out not even smelling like smoke.

When I have been in the most desperate times of my life, I have experienced and come to know God and His loving hand. When it seemed that I could not live another minute, God showed up and gave me strength to get through.

When the most precious treasures in my life were taken from me, I wanted to die, but God showed up and empowered me to live another day. When you love something so much that you do not think you can live without it, sometimes God will allow it to be taken from you just to show you that in Him you can do all things. *Do not put others or things before God, or you may have to go through this unbearable pain and suffering yourself . Seek first the Kingdom of God, and His righteousness and all these things shall be added to you* (Matthew 6:33).

Now it is time to move to my life's lessons. It will not take you long to see why I love Jesus so much.

Chapter 2
The Glass House

As the prison bus drove up to the Cofield Unit in Tennessee Colony, Texas (also known as "The Glass House" because the exterior was all glass), fear gripped my heart.

This is the one prison that other inmates said you do not want to go to. It is a maximum-security prison in which almost all inmates—murderers, rapists, child molesters and other hardened criminals—are spending 50 years to life without the chance for parole. I was not supposed to go to this prison. Because of a recent riot there, many inmates had been shipped away. Now they had to fill the beds. Just my luck!

The Cofield Unit had 3,000 inmates, the most in any prison unit in the state of Texas. The place was overcrowded, which made for more problems. This particular unit housed adseq and superseq. These were areas for the most dangerous of all criminals. Eventually I would get to feed them. After getting off the bus, we were brought in the back doors for assignments, bedding, sheets, and haircuts. Yes, they really shaved our heads!

We were then escorted to our new cells/homes. I can still remember all the whistling at us and the words "Hey, pretty boy." My fear grew a little more intense.

Once I got to my cell, I met my new cellmate. I soon

found out that he was a convicted child molester. He liked little boys. I thought to myself, *How in the world did I end up with this guy?* Today, I realize that God had set it all up. God sees the end from the beginning. You see, 15 years later a relative at a young age would be sexually abused. To prepare me for this trauma God wanted early on to teach me forgiveness.

I tried everything to get moved away from this guy, but was not successful. So I spent the next six months getting to know him. Actually, he was a very brilliant man. He was very sorry for what he had done. He had been sexually abused as a little boy. Thank God I had come to know the Lord as my Savior just a week before; otherwise I would not have had the compassion I felt for him. I actually tried to protect this man from others. We went to church together and spent many long nights talking about all we had both been through.

God knew whom I would be living with long before I got there. Psalm 139:16 says, *Your eyes saw my substance being yet unformed. And in Your book they all were written, the days fashioned for me, when as yet there were none of them.* God was preparing my heart by allowing this man to become a part of my life. Because of this man, I would be able to forgive the one who would eventually hurt my relative many years later. *God is so good.*

God used me to help this man come to know Jesus Christ as his personal Lord and Savior. I believe today that he is living a quality life.

Now it was time to go to work in the kitchen. Thank God I did not have to work in the fields. There were a lot of problems out there. God had mercy on me and showed me favor. My title in the kitchen was "cups and wipes." I would put out the cups and then pick them up. After everyone was finished, I would wipe the tables. So this was a good way to tell people about Jesus, because I was able to be in contact with others, one on one. Over the next six months I would get very involved in the church and Bible studies. I would build relationships. I would realize that there are good people in prison who just made bad decisions. Most of them were under the influence of drugs or alcohol when they committed their crimes. Most of them had no father figure. Although I never thought it could happen to me, I thanked God I got caught when I did. If not for God's grace, I would have died or gone insane before He rescued me. My life was spiraling out of control.

After six months in The Glass House, a friend of mine was raped in another inmate's cell. Then I heard the rapist was after me. I was scared and cried out to God, "Please get me off this farm." The next day I was called out of my cell and told I was being transferred. I did not care where I was going as long as I was getting away from this convict, who had been locked up 30 years or so.

I was transferred to the Venus Pre-Release Unit in Venus, Texas. Wow! God had spared me again. I cannot tell you how happy I was not to have to come face to face with that predator who had raped my friend.

I was about to see the favor of God in action in Venus, Texas.

Chapter 3
Favor in Venus

As I arrived at Venus Pre-Release, I could not help but think about Joseph in the Bible. He had favor wherever he went. God had shown me so much favor—now more than ever, by getting me out of The Glass House, where it was so hot that inmates constantly needed showers. The reflection of the sun off that glass was unbearable. Best of all, I was transferred before getting raped. I now was in a place that was more like a country club than a prison.

From day one I was shown favor. I was given the best job on the farm, working for the bosses and away from the inmate population. I was able to read my Bible, pray, go to church, watch TV, sing—do whatever I wanted to do. Freedom! The bosses would even bring us food from outside the prison. On the weekends I worked visitation. This duty consisted of popping popcorn and taking pictures for inmates and their families. I got to tell people about Jesus. I met my new girlfriend of the next year. Pretty cool, huh? I also went to school and got counseling during the year I was there. A lot of healing took place at Venus.

This is the place where I truly forgave my dad for all the abuse he had inflicted on me. Once in a group meeting, we got in a circle and put one empty chair in the middle. Then we were to confront the one who had abused us. It really worked. I am now free of all the hate and lack of forgiveness I had had toward my father.

Then it was time to deal with the anger I had toward the judge in Dallas whom I believe—although I, of course will never be totally sure—had blackballed me. I firmly believe he had told me I was getting 10 years' deferred-adjudicated probation. At sentencing, however, he gave me 20 years in the Texas Department of Corrections. The ecstasy drug I was busted with was not real. I believe the judge knew that if we went to trial, we would win the case. I believe that would have been the technicality that would have set me free. The judge said to bypass a jury trial. After being locked up 13 months, I was finally bench-warranted back to Dallas to go before the same judge. My attorney called the judge to the stand to testify. He recused himself. This means he chose to take himself off the case and would not testify.

We were assigned a new judge, who said he would let me out that day and start all over, or he would reduce my sentence to 15 years. My attorney suggested I take the 15 years and hopefully get out in 18 months, so I agreed.

I was now freer behind bars than people in the free world. I was so blessed and favored in this place called prison. I completely forgave the judge whom I have a strong suspicion had wronged me. That was very important in my healing process. Thank God I got caught. God was in control of my life. I would never be the same.

After a year in Venus, I was given a one-week furlough to go to my mother's house, find a church, and get adjusted. This was a miracle in itself. Not many people get furloughs, especially those who had been imprisoned on drug charges. I met Randy Richter of Law of Liberty Ministries. He took me under his wing, gave me a van, and discipled me when I was released. This relationship would not have come about if God had not blessed me with this furlough.

Then I went back to Venus for a week, said my goodbyes, and walked out the door to freedom on July 5, 1991. When I walked out the doors at Venus, I began to weep. Over the past year I had built many friendships there. By the time I arrived at my mother's home, I was already missing the people I had grown to know spiritually.

I had nothing when I got out of prison, but it seemed I had everything. No amount of money can buy family, peace, joy, friends, health and most of all love. Once I was at my mother's home, I began to reflect over the past 17 months and 23 days.

All of a sudden I remembered how I had told God that if he would get me out of prison in less than 18 months, I would serve Him the rest of my life. Inmates told me I was crazy when I told them that God would answer my prayers. But because God reduced my sentence to 15 years and backdated nine days of jail time at the last minute, I was released at 17 months and 23 days. God is so good. I was free at last, but would it last?

Chapter 4
A New Life (I Thought)

For the next two years, I served God and loved people. I gave my testimony and preached in churches. This was great and had been my dream ever since God changed my life.

For two years I surrounded myself with the right people and remained accountable to Randy Richter of Law of Liberty Ministries. But the day arrived when an old friend asked me to go to a birthday party at a nightclub. I thought, "No problem, I am strong enough that no temptation can overtake me." Pride set in. Before I knew it, I had gone to the party with a friend from the past and taken a drink that turned into many drinks. On the way home I hit a curb. The next thing I knew flashing red lights were behind me. Unbelievably, in all my years of drinking and drugging, I had never been pulled over. Now I was given a breath test and then taken to jail. I hired an attorney and was given three year's probation. Thank God my parole was not revoked. Favor again. God has been so good to me.

So now I am on parole and probation. Not many people can say that! You would have thought this would get my attention. Well, it did for about six months or so until I met a woman at a nightclub. She was a beautiful California girl. We began to date and became engaged.

We then did cocaine together. As sin always does, it brings death or destruction. It was not long before I was asked to take a drug test at probation. Well, you guessed it; I flunked it. Instead of going in to face it, I went on the run for three months of pure hell on earth. I continued doing cocaine in great amounts. I had a cardiac arrest while lying in bed one night after doing too much of it. I remember wanting to die, but God would not let me, since He holds my every breath in His hand. Finally, after this, I called my mother and oldest brother, Alan, and asked them to take me to Lew Sterrett Jail in Dallas, Texas. I wanted to turn myself in. Another near-death experience and all the paranoia and destruction of those around me finally brought unbearable guilt.

By the grace of God, instead of revoking my parole and sending me back to prison, the judge sent me to a drug-rehabilitation facility in downtown Houston, Texas, for six months. This was another of God's favors!

I went to drug classes and school. After three months I rebelled against one of the teachers, so I was put in "solitary confinement" (a cell with only a steel bed, sink, shower and commode). I could have no visits or contact with anyone. My cell was a dark 5-by-7 room with a small glass window in the door. Here I hit bottom again. I decided I wanted to hang myself with my jail clothes.

Before attempting to kill myself, something deep inside me cried out to God one more time, *"God, if you are real, please show yourself to me."* Within a minute or so, a card came sliding in my cell underneath the door. I opened it. It was the "Footprints in the Sand" card. I read it until I got to the part that said, "When you only

see one set of footprints, it was there that I carried you."
I fell to my knees on the steel bed, crying like a baby, knowing that God had invaded that small dark room with His presence because He loved me so much and still had a plan for my life. My whole attitude changed. I made it through until I was released to go home and try again.

Thank God I got caught before I took my life and ended up in eternal hell. What an awesome God we serve. But will this encounter be enough to get me through on the outside? Let's find out!

Chapter 5
Lukewarm Brings Bondage

After serving my time in Houston, I was on my way to my mother's house. I thought to myself, "I will never go back again." I went into business and immediately started making money in construction. Before I knew it, I was so busy making money that I was not spending a lot of time with God. I began to love money and the world more than God. At this time I was riding the fence—one leg in the world and one leg serving God. Revelation 3:16 says, *So then, because you are lukewarm, and neither cold or hot, I will vomit you out of My mouth.* No wonder I was miserable, complaining, and angry at the world. No wonder no one wanted what I had. I would play games with God over the next few years before a thought came to my mind. *"What are you doing?"* I thought for the first time in my life. *"What am I here for?"* I was so lonely on the inside. I really did not have any friends to speak of. I felt afraid and lonely.

In relationships I found myself treating women the same way my dad treated my mother. He was mentally and emotionally abusive. I hated my dad for what he had done to my mother and me. How ironic then that I found myself being just like him. Paul said in Romans 7:15, *For what I am doing, I do not understand. For what I will to do, that I do not practice; but what I hate, that I do.*

What we see and hear as children is what we become until we receive Christ into our hearts by being born again. And then and only then does hope for change occur.

So here I am, saved, going to heaven when I die, but still miserable. I was trying to love God and people. Really, I wanted to serve God and be what He wanted me to be, but the world still got the best of me. All I cared about was sleeping with the next woman, making more money, and being accepted. I did not care who I stepped on, lied to, or deceived. I cared only about Clark and what I thought was best for me. All the while, my heart was getting harder and harder. I began not to even feel anything—nor did I have a conscience. A few more years went by and finally I met someone in church that I was just crazy about. The only problem was that she was married. I can hear you laughing now. Even crazier than that, is that at this time I was the youth pastor at a church in Dallas, Texas. It did not take long for the lust of my eyes and the lust of my flesh to bring me down. Within a few weeks, I fell into the sin of adultery, sleeping with a married woman. I was asked to resign my position as youth pastor. The woman and I decided to split up. She went back to her husband. We both really just wanted what was right.

She was gone from my life for a month or so until she returned. Meanwhile, the pastor had reinstated me as youth pastor and given me a second chance. But you guessed it—when this woman came back, the lust in my heart was greater than my love for God. We fell back into sin, mostly because of me. She was new to the Lord.

I would use the Word as a hammer to do whatever I willed. I was asked by the pastor to resign, so I did. One of the toughest things I had to do at the time was stand up and face all the youth and their parents. I had to explain what I had done. How humiliating! I can just imagine how many lives were shattered because of my sin. You see, until you and I let God into our hearts and deal with the real root issues, we will continue to do the things we hate, even at the expense of the ones we love the most. Our sin affects all those around us—in most cases the ones that we love the most. Our families often are damaged the most.

For the next three years I lived in willful sin. I lived a roller coaster life of love, hate and deception. I thought I was the woman's savior. What a dangerous place to live! We really wanted to get married, but her husband would not give her a divorce. This relationship would continue until two-and-a-half years later when she became pregnant with our son, Conner. Five months later she got her divorce.

I was very happy about the divorce, as there had been a long journey of pain and suffering to get to this point. Romans 6:23 says, *For the wages of sin is death.* I thought the pain and suffering would finally stop, but it had just begun. You see, our foundation was not built on the rock of Jesus Christ. It was built on sin. However, we were married three years after meeting.

I started ministering every chance I could, even though I had not dealt with some deep-rooted issues. I ministered on TV and radio and in churches, under tents, on the streets, in hospitals, in grocery stores and anywhere else possible. Once at the corner of Ferguson Road and Highland Road in Dallas, Texas, when Pastor Jimmy Clark and I were discipling/ministering to some new converts on how to win souls, gunshots started going off. Gang members were shooting over our heads. Before it was all said and done, a number of them were lined up in front of a convenience store giving their lives to Jesus Christ. *Glory to God in the highest.* You see the most dangerous place to be is not among gangs, but outside the will of God. He said, *"No weapon formed against you shall prosper"* (Isaiah 54:17). If God is for you, who can be against you?

Nothing is better than leading someone to Jesus Christ. I repeat, nothing is better than helping someone else. Nothing is better than loving someone who is in need. We must live to give. Our lives are not for us, but for others. What you make happen for others, God will make happen for you. One of the greatest things you can do is go to hospitals, nursing homes, and orphanages and give your life away. Give your time away. Love people. Hurting people are everywhere. Someone has a worse situation than you do. People may be smiling on the outside, but God sees their hearts. If He puts compassion in your heart for someone, then He is telling you to go to him or her. You have what the person needs. Be faithful to God. He will show you what to do. Just go and be obedient.

The spirit of the Lord God is upon me, because the Lord has anointed me to preach the gospel to the poor; He has sent Me to heal the broken hearted, to proclaim liberty to the captives, and recovery of sight to the blind, to set at liberty those who are oppressed, and to proclaim the acceptable year of the Lord (Isaiah 61:1-2). It is time for each of us to rise up and let God be God in each of us. Are you a willing vessel?

You might be saying, "I am not ready. I am still a mess. I will when I get healed." Well, today is the day of salvation. Your healing will come as you seek God and start helping others. Get your eyes off yourself. God is for you; He wants to use you where you are.

My marriage went on for another nine years before we separated. We never dealt with the issues that could have saved our marriage. We tried, but it just did not seem to work. I do not believe in divorce outside of adultery, so my wife had no biblical grounds against me. I was always faithful to her, but things just did not work well. God has used this difficult situation in my life for His glory and my good. I am telling you this because I put off ministry for years because I believed that God could not use me in this condition. I was so miserable because I was not loving people and telling people about Jesus. I have been condemned because of my marital situation, but you do not have to be. Let God use you right where you are. He has a plan for your life. It starts right where you are. Do not let the devil steal one more day, month or year from you.

Now let's move on to the greatest days of our lives. *Old things are passed away, and all things have become new* (2 Corinthians 5:17).

Chapter 6
Addicted to Jesus

A place in God will satisfy every need you have. Apart from God, the Bible says, "We can do nothing." One thing I have learned over all the years of addiction, separation, divorce, gambling, abuse, hate, bitterness, unforgiveness, jealousy, possessiveness, control and everything else the devil represents is that God Himself through Christ Jesus, by the power of the Holy Spirit, is the only way to become free. The Bible says that whom the Son sets free is free indeed. Only Christ Jesus can set you free. He went to the Cross and paid the price for the world's sin. He took your place and my place. He awaits your surrender of your life.

My healing process did not begin until I totally surrendered everything to Jesus. Today I am free and free indeed. I am not just living life, but life more abundantly. This book is being written 19 years after I came to Jesus Christ. It has taken me a long time to get free, not because of Jesus, but because of my stubbornness. Please learn from my mistakes, pain, and suffering so that you will not have to go down the road I did.

I thank God for all of it. If it were not for my mistakes, you and others would not be hearing God's truth today. Maybe my mistakes are the very things that will get your name into the Lamb's Book of Life. We overcome the devil by the blood of the Lamb and the word of our testimony. The reason I am writing this book is that maybe someone will relate to my life story and will receive Jesus as his or her Lord and Savior. There is hope for you.

God loves you so much, and so do I. He desires for you to be happy more than you yourself wish to be happy. He created you for Himself. You are so special to God. He says that you are the apple of His eye. His thoughts toward you are more in number than the sand (Psalm 139:18). He holds your very tears in a bottle. He knows where you are today. He knows every place you hurt. He wants to restore everything to you that the devil has stolen. When He does, it will be bigger, better, greater and beyond what you could ever ask or think (Ephesians 3:20). He desires restoration for your life more than you do.

Jeremiah 29:11 says, *For I know the thoughts I have towards you, says the Lord, thoughts of peace and not of evil, to give you a future and a hope.* His plan for your life is great. Do not look at where you are today, but where you can be in a year from now. God wants your heart. Give it to Him today and watch what God will do for you. Your life will turn out to be beyond your wildest dreams if you will just trust Him. He has changed my life in a way that I could never have dreamed. Today I walk by faith and not by sight. I am grounded and rooted in love. Peace rules and reigns in my heart. I live to give. My thoughts are not on my problems but on whom I can help today. I used to be the most selfish person you could ever know. My family will vouch for that! It is not as if I do not have a reason to be depressed, complaining, blaming God, hating my enemies, etc. I have been stripped of my children, job, car, possessions and reputation. I was recently jailed and extradited to Dallas, Texas. The truth is, God allowed these experiences in order to bring me to where I am today. *I have been crucified with Christ; nevertheless I live, yet not I, but Christ in me* (Galatians 2:20). The truth has already come out. As I write this book things are being restored.

You see, through the tough times we see who we truly are. How do you react when the pressure comes? Do you turn to alcohol or drugs? Do you overcome evil with good, or do you try to get even? Are you jealous, possessive or controlling? Do you have a temper? Are you the one who lifts one finger to someone who cuts you off on the highway? Do you curse without realizing it until it is too late? I used to answer, "yes" to all those questions. Thank God I allowed Jesus into my heart. I had suppressed so much hate in my heart over the years and covered it up with drugs, alcohol, sex, prescription pills, etc., but thanks be to God, He has set me free. He wants to do the same for you. He will not violate your will, though. He awaits your surrender. Will you call on Him now and let Him begin the process? It will be the greatest decision you could make outside of being born again. It will not only change you, but your family, friends and others as well.

Now can you see why I titled this book *Thank God I Got Caught*? The very things the devil tries to destroy us with are the very things that God will use to change you, and the world—and has used to change me. In Genesis 50:20 Joseph said to his brothers, *"You meant it for evil against me, but God meant it for good. In order to bring it about as it is this day to save many people's lives."* Are you one of these people?

Chapter 7
Love Eternal

I want to tell you about the greatest gift of all—LOVE! From my heart to yours, I yearn for you to experience the love of God, because this love is why I am who I am today. It took me many years to understand how a loving God could let me be so hurt and suffer so much pain. Please listen carefully so that you can be healed and receive by faith God's love for you.

Romans 8:38,39 says, *For I am persuaded that neither death nor life, nor angels nor principalities nor powers, nor things present nor things to come, nor height, nor depth, nor any other created thing, shall be able to separate us from the love of God which is in Christ Jesus our Lord.* Friends, nothing you have done or ever could do can separate you from the love of God. He loves you unconditionally. He has a plan for your life. That plan is beyond anything you could ever imagine. If you will trust Him and allow Him into your heart to do what He wants to do, you will one day be grateful. Your family will be grateful. Everyone you come in contact with will be grateful.

God's love can melt the hardest heart. I can vouch for that! His love will cause you to love the unlovely, to forgive the people who hurt you the most. His love will unlock the door of forgiveness in your heart. Everything good comes from God's love.

1 Corinthians 13:13 says, *And now abide faith, hope, love, these three, but the greatest of these is love.*

1 Corinthians 13:8 says, *Love never fails.* I am proof. Because of love, I have been able to forgive others who have hurt me or ones I love. This could never have happened if I had not received God's love. Because of love I was able to forgive my father for all he did to me. Because of love I was able to forgive the friend who did not do me right. Because of love I forgave the judge I felt wronged me. Because of love I was able to forgive myself and love myself in a healthy way. Because of love I now spend most of my time in hospitals, nursing homes, orphanages and other places of need, praying and serving people who are hurting. I live to give. My purpose is to help other people become all they can be. Wow! This is a far cry from who I was for many years. God's love transformed my life. Thank God I am a servant. Thank God I got caught many years ago. We must decide that we will serve God even if we never get what we want. Like Job, we must say, *Though He slay me, yet will I trust Him* (Job 13:15).

God has actually done more for me since the time I totally surrendered my will to His than He had ever done previously. However, I did go through a time of testing in which I had to seek Him simply for Himself and not for anything He might give me.

Because of God's love for me, He has delivered me from all my fears. He has saved me from all my troubles. He has delivered me out of the hand of all my enemies.

He will do the same for you.

Psalm 34:19 says, *Many are the afflictions of the righteous, but the Lord delivers him out of them all.* Isn't this good news? God has always been faithful to me, and He will do the same for you if you will trust Him with your life. He loved you so much that He sent His Son Jesus to die for you. He shed His blood for your sins. He has set you free. All you have to do is receive by faith His love. You will never be the same.

My life story is summed up in Psalm 40:1-3: *I waited patiently for the Lord; and He inclined to me, and heard my cry. He also brought me up out of a horrible pit, out of the miry clay, and set my feet upon a rock, and established my steps. He has put a new song in my mouth-Praise to our God: Many will see it and fear, and will trust in the Lord.*

What an awesome God we serve. Please surrender your life to the One who created you. He longs to be your Father and best friend. He desires for you to be happy and have life more abundantly here on earth. He has never left you or forsaken you. He has always been there for you. He is the reason you are still alive and have breath today.

I pray that you will get addicted to walking in love and blessing people. Thank God I got caught 20 years ago, because today I am alive to give you hope and life in Jesus Christ, the lover of your soul. Now join me in saying, "Lord, thank God I got caught by your love today!"

Chapter 8
Fear of Failure

The reason most people fail is fear! You must be willing to step out of the boat when God tells you to. God has placed dreams in each of our hearts. But because of fear we stay right where we are. We have been hurt so many times in the past that we have become paralyzed by our feelings. We would rather stay in an abusive relationship than change, because we become comfortable. Fear is, "false evidence appearing real."

Most of the time we fear things that would never happen. Yet because we believe it will happen, it does happen. You believe fear into existence the same way faith is activated. Hebrews 11:1 says, *Now faith is the substance of things hoped for, the evidence of things not seen.* Faith activates God, and fear activates the devil. The time is now to trust God and believe in Him. My life and circumstances changed when I began to believe that God is bigger than my circumstances and problems. When you trust God with all your heart, fear begins to dwindle and then disappear.

2 Corinthians 10:4-5 says, *For the weapons of our warfare are not carnal but mighty in God for pulling down strongholds, casting down vain imaginations and every high thing that exalts itself against the knowledge of God, bringing every thought into captivity to the obedi-*

ence of Christ.

Remember, everything begins with a thought. Your mind is the devil's playground until you renew it with the word of God. In the next chapter I will tell you how to renew your mind. John 4:18 says, *There is no fear in love, but perfect love casts out fear, because fear involves torment.*

2 Timothy 1:7 says, *For God has not given us a spirit of fear, but of power and of love and of a sound mind.*

As a young boy my father emotionally abused me. I lived in total fear for about 20 year. It was embedded in my heart and mind. I feared my father, relationships, failing in sports, school, talking in front of people, being accepted and many other things. I never knew what love was. I looked at God the same way I saw my father. That is why it is so important for fathers to love your children, to be patient and kind to them, to accept them just the way they are. Abuse is rampant in families today, but God can and will change that.

To be honest, just recently I have learned to walk by faith and not out of fear. You do not have to fear failure or people anymore. God loves you! God loves you! God loves you! Repeat this over and over every day until you believe it, because perfect love (God's love) casts out fear. God loves me! God loves me! God loves me! He has a plan for your life. Do not live by feelings and emotions. Live by faith in the Son of God. Jesus shed His precious blood for you so that you can be saved and not live by fear, but by faith.

Remember that whatever you believe will come to pass—whether you live by faith or fear. Faith activates

God, and fear activates the devil. In John 10:10 Jesus says, *"The thief does not come except to steal, and to kill, and to destroy. I have come that they may have life, and that they may have it more abundantly."* I can tell you that I am living life more abundantly. My life in Christ is greater than I could ever have imagined. Thank God he delivered me from fear of man and circumstances. God is fighting all my battles. He wants to fight yours, too. God is for you. If He is for you, then who can be against you?

1 John 3:8 says that Jesus came to destroy the works of the devil. Let Him destroy the works of the devil in you. Let Him destroy the fear in you. He will replace it with His perfect love. What an incredible love it is.

In Luke 19:10 Jesus said, *"For the Son of Man (Jesus Christ) has come to seek and to save that which was lost." If you will seek Him with all your heart, He will save you from all your fear. Whom the Son sets free, will be free indeed.*

This is your day to be free from the torment of fear once and for all. Pray, **"Lord, come into my life and take the fear out of my heart. Replace it with your perfect love. I repent of living in fear. I thank you for cleansing me in your precious blood now. Amen!"**

Chapter 9
Renewing Your Mind

I want to tell you how to renew your mind. Everything you do starts with a thought. You can either accept it, or as we talked about in the last chapter, you can cast it down and replace it with the Word of God.

Philippians 4:8 says, *Finally, brethren, whatever things are noble, whatever things are just, whatever things are pure, whatever things are lovely, whatever things are of good report, if there is any virtue and if there is anything praiseworthy, meditate on these things.*

I remember when I was in prison, especially in solitary confinement, that the plan to commit suicide first entered my mind. Thank God something deep within me cried out, "God, if you are real, please show yourself to me." He did by sending that "footprints in the sand" card under the door; otherwise I would not be here today. The point is that suicide, murder, rage, unforgiveness, hate, anger, rape, etc., all start with a thought. I never did drugs until I thought about it first. I never took a drink until I thought about it first. I never attempted suicide until I thought about it first. Everything starts with a thought. The temptations will come, but God gives you the power to cast those thoughts down immediately and replace them with His word.

When Jesus was in the wilderness 40 days and was

tempted by Satan, what did He do? Luke 4:4 tells us that Jesus answered him, *"Man shall not live by bread alone, but by every word of God."* In Luke 4:8 Jesus said, *"Get behind me, Satan!' For it is written, 'you shall worship the Lord your God, and Him only you shall serve.'"*

Jesus answered in Luke 4:12, *"It has been said, 'You shall not tempt the Lord your God.'"* Study the word of God. Know the word of God. When a wrong thought comes, say, "For it is written;" then speak the word of God. It works for me; it will work for you! You will be amazed how your life will change. James 1:14-15 says, *But each one is tempted when he is drawn away by his own desires and enticed. Then, when desire has conceived, it gives birth to sin; and sin, when it is full grown, brings forth death.*

This means that when the thought comes, if you do not cast it down and replace it with God's Word, then the desire is conceived (becomes real) and it becomes sin. And the wages of sin is death. Beloved let God renew your mind. Let go of the things that are destroying your marriage, hurting your children, hurting your relationships and most of all destroying your own life. God loves you and wants to heal your every hurt. Open your heart to Him today. Give Him your mind, and He will give you the mind of Christ. You will begin to think like Him, act like Him, worship like Him, pray like Him, and love like Him. Your marriage will be renewed. Your relationships with your children will be renewed.

What I would have given to know these truths in my marriage years ago. Maybe things would not have ended up as they are now. But if my pain and suffering through it all helps you and your family, then it will have all been worth it.

Numbers 6:24-26 says, *May the Lord bless you and keep you; May the Lord make His face shine upon you, and be gracious to you; May the Lord lift up His countenance upon you, and give you peace.*

Chapter 10
From Prisoner to Worshiper

I want to encourage you to do something that will not only benefit you, but will honor our heavenly Father and His Son. Worship!! It will change you forever! The Bible says God inhabits the praises of His people. Psalm 100:4 says, *Enter His gates with thanksgiving and His courts with praise*. This is our way of thanking Him for all He has done, is doing, and will do for us.

Psalm 103:1-5 says, *Bless the Lord, O my soul; and all that is within me, bless His holy name! Bless the Lord, O my soul, and forget not all His benefits: Who forgives all your iniquities, Who heals all your diseases, Who redeems your life from destruction, Who crowns you with loving kindness and tender mercies, Who satisfies your mouth with good things, so that your youth is renewed like the eagles*. Wow! What an awesome God we serve.

How can you not worship and praise Him? How can you not give your life to Him? He is the lover of your soul. He is the One who has given you the power to get wealth. He is the one who died for you. He is the One who has healed you or can heal you. He is the One who has brought your life out of destruction or will bring your life up out of the horrible pit you are in. You have no hope apart from Jesus Christ. Unless one is born again, he cannot see the kingdom of God. Jesus Christ is the way, the truth, and the life; no man or woman comes to the Father except through Jesus.

Are you as fired up as I am? Do you sense the Holy Spirit of God right now? He is drawing you right now to surrender your life to Him. Praise Him and worship Him right now. Say, "Jesus, I love You, I praise You, I worship You for who You are. You have been so good to me. You have blessed me with my health, children, husband or wife, home, car, water, electricity, my sight and everything else that is good. Thank you, Jesus, for dying on the cross for me. Thank you for shedding Your blood so I can be forgiven of my sins. Thank you that I have breath today. Thank you I am not laid up in a hospital bed today." If you are in the hospital or sick, say, "Thank you, Lord, for healing my body and giving me another day. Thank you that I am not living on the streets." We have so much to be thankful for. Stop complaining! Start worshiping Him for all He has done for you. It works! God is faithful! God loves you! God has a plan for your life. Glory to God in the highest!

If anybody knows that times can get difficult, it is I. But I want to tell you that God has always been faithful to me. Often patience was needed in my circumstances, but the answer always came. Time and again I was brought up out of deep places that would have swallowed me without God. But it has produced a confidence in my heart that I am told shows all over my face. People have asked me, "How can you worship God in the situations you find yourself in?" I answer them this way: "I never cast away my confidence in the faithfulness of God." I just start remembering all the times He showed up in my life to save me. I just begin to thank Him and worship Him. Then something just happens that I cannot put into words. All I can say is, "Thank God I got caught by Him. I once was a prisoner, but now I am a worshiper. Glory to God!"

2 Chronicles 7:14 says, *If My people who are called by My name will humble themselves, and pray and seek My face, and turn from their wicked ways, then I will hear from heaven, and will forgive their sin and heal their land.*

Now will you say with me, **"Thank God I got caught by the living God?"** If you said these words, your life and family will never be the same. To God be the glory!

Chapter 11
Clark Crawford Ministries

In closing I would like to tell you about the birthing of Clark Crawford Ministries. In one of my upcoming books, *Extradited*, you will see why Clark Crawford was "extradited" from Fresno, California to Dallas, Texas, on November 17, 2008, to preach the gospel of Jesus Christ. There will be no denying that Clark was "set-up" for a great and mighty "comeback". This is where Clark Crawford Ministries was birthed.

In this closing chapter I would like to tell you of the many things that have taken place in the past two months regarding Clark Crawford Ministries. When I returned to Dallas, Texas, I needed a haircut so my younger brother, Rich, referred me to Ben Sarratt. I went to see him. He asked me to visit him at First Family Church in Dallas. I took him up on his offer. I can tell you that the blessings of God have run me down and overtaken me since the day I walked through those doors. I walked into the arms of the most loving and compassionate people I have ever experienced inside the walls of a church. The pastor took me in and has never stopped loving me. He speaks words that are living, powerful, and sharper than any two-edged sword—*piercing even to the division of soul and spirit, and of joints and marrow, and is a discerner of the thoughts and intents of the heart* (Hebrews 4:12). Thank God I met Ben Sarratt and went to First Family Church. His obedience and boldness to ask me to come to church opened the floodgates of heaven concerning Clark and Clark Crawford Ministries.

In December 2008 the Lord moved on my heart to go get a post office box for mail. On my way to the post office the Lord spoke "Clark Crawford Ministries" into my heart. So I opened up the post office box with the name of Clark Crawford Ministries. A few days later I received a call from one of my best friends, Pastor Jimmy Clark of Dallas. He said, "Clark, I feel like the Lord is saying for you to go open a post office box in the name of Clark Crawford Ministries." *Glory to God!*

Then a few weeks later I started receiving mail from people I had written in prison. These people told me how their lives were changed forever as a result of a few kind words written to them in their time of need.

Also, in just a few short weeks, my first book, *Thank God I Got Caught* would be completed. The Lord brought me a manuscript typist, an editor, and a publisher. Everything is coming together. What the enemy meant for harm, the Lord has turned for good. Joseph told his brothers, *but as for you, you meant evil against me; but God meant it for good, in order to bring it about as it is this day, to save many people alive* (Genesis 50:20). *All things work together for good to those who love God and are called according to His purpose* (Romans 8:28).

In just a few short weeks, I humbly tell you, we are now going into two nursing homes in Mesquite, Texas, Texas Youth Commission in Dallas, Texas, doing Bible studies, and taking orphans out to play games and eat pizza on a monthly basis from Buckner's Orphanage, as well as, doing Bible studies for 13 different Angel Houses throughout the DFW area. This does not include the churches, over-comers groups and other ministry functions we are doing. We serve an awesome God who is looking for surrendered and available servants. Thank God He brought me back to Dallas, Texas.

The Lord has brought me an administrator, John Robertson, a publicist, as well as other team members. He is continuing to make a way where there seemed to be none. The Lord has brought the finances for everything we need, and much more.

By now you have read "Clark's Journal: Angel Visitation" in the beginning of this book; God will even send you angels to deliver finances and groceries if He has to. As Joyce Meyer says, "God will make bananas grow off telephone poles if He has to." Isn't that great!!

Who would have ever thought I would be writing books? I did not know anything about writing, but God tells you to do things that you are not capable of doing without Him. If you will just obey when God tells you to do what you think is impossible, He will give you the ability to walk it out. As I began to write this book, it was as though the Lord breathed upon it. He inspired this book the same way He inspired other men to write the Bible. Thank you Lord. I am so grateful and humbled by what You are doing in me and through me.

I humbly tell you, Clark Crawford and Clark Crawford Ministries have been prophesied over to be on every major television and radio station around the world.

This is a confirming word from the 1990s. *For the vision is yet for an appointed time, but at the end it will speak, and it will not lie. Though it tarries, wait for it, because it will surely come, it will not tarry* (Habakkuk 2:3).

Just in the last month we have been asked to go on television. We are waiting for the dates and times right now. Please visit our website at *www.clarkcrawfordministries.com* to find out up-to-date information about our ministry. You can also sign up to receive our newsletter, purchase books, view a calendar of events and more. We are so humbled and thankful to our Lord and Savior for what He is doing in and through us.

My dreams are so big. God has shown me things that I cannot tell anyone. They would think I am crazy, but I serve an awesome God. He is able to do exceedingly abundantly above all that we can ask or even think, according to the power (Holy Spirit) who works in us (Ephesians 3:20). With God all things are possible (Matthew 19:26). Do not limit God. He wants to do the impossible in you, through you, and all around you.

Remember all the times God has saved you from all your fears, from the hand of all your enemies, and out of all your troubles. Give Him praise and glory right now. Thank Him for His goodness in your life. We have so much to be thankful for. Get your eyes off your circumstances and get them on your God. He is the way-maker. He makes a way where there seems to be no way. He makes a road in the wilderness and rivers in the desert (Isaiah 43:19). Get fired up and go make a difference in your world today. He loves you so much that He died for you. You are awesome in and through Christ Jesus. He will do things that you have never dreamed of. All you have to do is trust Him, love Him, serve Him, and most of all, have a relationship with Him. God is more real to me than anyone here in the flesh. He lives in my heart and is a friend that sticks closer than a brother. He will never leave you nor forsake you. He awaits your surrender right now.

If you do not know Jesus Christ as your Lord and Savior, please pray the "salvation prayer" at the end of this book (under the "I Want to Hear From You" section). All you have to do is ask Jesus Christ into your heart, repent of your sins, and you will be saved. He desires a relationship with you—not religion, which gives rules and laws. He came to give you life and life more abundantly. It is not by works, but by grace. You can never earn it or work for it; Jesus has already paid the price for you. Will you give your life to Him right now? It will be the greatest decision you have ever made. I love you all.

Upcoming Books

Thank God For My Enemies

This book will be in print by the end of June 2009. Clark Crawford has been reduced to love because of his enemies. Clark has learned the real meaning of forgiveness, because of some recent events. In (Genesis 50:20) Joseph said to his brothers, (who sold him into slavery) *"but as for you, you meant it for evil against me; but God meant it for good, in order to bring it about as it is this day, to save many people alive"*.

Clark has learned first hand: (Matthew 5:44) *But I say to you, love your enemies, bless those who curse you, do good to those who hate you, and pray for those who spitefully use you and persecute you.*

You will look at your enemies in a whole different light after reading this power-packed book inspired by God.

Extradited

More details about this book will be made known on our website in the near future. Find out how and why Clark Crawford was "extradited" from Fresno, California, to Dallas, Texas, to preach the gospel of Jesus Christ. There will be no denying that Clark was "set-up" for a great and mighty "comeback."

Sixteen Days in Solitary Confinement

More details about this book will be made known on our website in the near future. Find out how being alone with God and the Bible in a dark, 5-by-7 cell caused an encounter that would forever change Clark Crawford's divine destiny.

I WANT TO HEAR FROM YOU!

At the end of every message I preach, I give individuals in the audience an opportunity to make Jesus Christ the Lord of their lives. I would like to extend that same opportunity to you.

I am not talking about joining a church or finding religion. I am talking about finding life, peace and joy. Would you pray with me today? Just say, "Lord Jesus, I repent of my sins. I ask You to come into my heart and save me. I ask You to be Lord and Savior of my life."

Beloved, if you have prayed that simple prayer, I believe you have been born again. Your name has been written in the Lamb's Book of Life in heaven. You will spend eternity with God. This is the greatest decision you have ever made.

I encourage you to get involved in a Bible-based church and keep God in first place in your life.

I love you and I will be praying for you. I also would love to hear from you!

To contact me, write to: Clark Crawford Ministries
P.O. Box 570131
Dallas, TX 75357

Or you can e-mail me at:
clark@clarkcrawfordministries.com

Remembering how you met the Lord is so very important. Write Your Testimony below and on the following page, then find someone with whom you can share it:

Now below make a list of all the things in your life that you need to pray about right now. Feel free to use the next blank pages, too. Find someone with whom you can share this list and ask them to pray for these things, too.

1.

2.

3.

4.

5.

6.

7.

8.

9.

10.

www.ingramcontent.com/pod-product-compliance
Lightning Source LLC
Chambersburg PA
CBHW052114070526
44584CB00017B/2486

THANK GOD I GOT CAUGHT

FROM PRISONER TO WORSHIPER

CLARK CRAWFORD

CrossHouse

Copyright by Clark Crawford, 2009
All Rights Reserved
Published by
CrossHouse Publishing,
P.O. Box 461592
Garland, Texas 75046-1592
Printed in the United States of America
by Lightning Source, LaVergne, TN

ISBN 978-1-934749-51-7
Library of Congress 2009925400